The Way Back:
Beyond Suburbia

Nana Ollerenshaw

To Maura,
With whom I share Washington (I have a brother there).
Best Wishes,
Nana

BeWrite Books

Published internationally by BeWrite Books, UK.
32 Bryn Road South, Wigan, Lancashire, WN4 8QR.

© Nana Ollerenshaw 2005

The right of Nana Ollerenshaw to be identified as the author has been asserted in accordance with sections 77 and 78 of the Copyright, Designs and Patents Act 1988. All rights reserved.

British Library Cataloguing in Publication Data. A catalogue record for this book is available from the British Library

ISBN 1-905202-20-2

Also available in eBook format

Produced by BeWrite Books

This book is sold subject to the condition that it shall not, by way of trade or otherwise, be lent, resold, hired out or otherwise circulated without the publisher's or author's consent in any form other than this current form and without a similar condition being imposed upon a subsequent purchaser. No part of this publication may be reproduced, stored in a retrieval system, or transmitted in any form by any means electronic, mechanical, photocopying, recording or otherwise without the permission of the publisher or author.

cover photographs © Nana Ollerenshaw

Acknowledgements:-
Some of these poems have previously been published. Thanks to...
'Encouragement Awards' (anthology), *'End of Season'* (anthology), *Jacobyte Poetry, 'Kaleidoscope'* (anthology), *'Lost in Thought'* (anthology), *The Select Six, Write News, Writer's Friend* and *Yellow Moon*

Biographical Note

Born Nana Carroll in New Haven, Connecticut, Nana Ollerenshaw obtained an Arts and a Master of Arts in Teaching degree, majoring in literature. At 22 she married an Australian and moved permanently to Australia. She taught at preschool, primary and secondary levels. Later she changed course and became an Endorsed Enrolled Nurse, practising in South Australia and currently in Queensland. She has three grown children and lives at Buderim on the Sunshine Coast with her husband.

Since starting to write poetry, Nana has won the open section of Laura Folk Fair's CJ Dennis Poetry Award 2004 and 2005, and first place in the Nature category of the Yellow Moon competition 2003, plus placings in many other poetry competitions. This is her first collection.

Dedication

to
Sally, Nancy and Evan.
To my mother, and my husband Stephen

Contents

Continent	13
The Glasshouse Mountains	14
Train Song	15
Boobook Owl	16
Bush	17
Kangaroo	18
Country Road	19
Fruit Bats	20
Lychee Madness	21
Flood	22
Outback Landscape	23
Christmas Bells at Mooloolah	24
Brush Turkey	25
Heat Wave	26
Monaro High Country	27
Cockatoo	28
Droughtv	29
St. Andrew's Cross Spider	30
Letting Go	31
Yellow-tailed Black Cockatoo	32
Men on Bikes	33
Budgerigar	34
Road Butterflies	35
Mount Coolum	36
Sea Change	37
Mackay	38
Jellyfish	39
The Farmhouse	40
The Rescue	41
Rock Pools	42
Mooloolaba	43
Snorkel	44
Ocean Swim	45

Ocean Race	46
The Deep	47
Seahorse	48
Late Love	49
Canberra in January 2003	50
Delivery	51
Pippa	52
Mystique	53
Upstairs Resident	54
The Way Back	55
Marital	56
Return	57
Yesterday's Bike Ride	58
Palace Centro	59
Stick Insect	60
Bird of Paradise Flower	61
Hummingbird	62
Rainstorm	63
Rainbow Lorrikeets	64
Love Story	65
On the Side	66
The Sausage Tree	67
The Parting	68
Conductor's Lament	69
The Piano Player	70
Sculpture	71
Fitness	72
Sprint	73
Medley	74
Between	75
Beyond Suburbia	76
At Taabinga Music Festival	77
Eclipse	78
King Parrot	79
Country on the Edge	80
Buff Banded Rail	81

Inside Binoculars	82
Corellas	83
The Prophecy	84
Flying	85
Trans Pacific	86
747	87
Subterranean	88
Jetlag	89
Summer House	90
The Grapes of Childhood	91
Aged	92
Depressed	93
My Mother's Rooms	94
Obese Woman	95
Lady with Oxygen	96
Heirarchy	97
Perspective	98
Old Man Dying	99
Night Patients	100
Surgery	101
Hospital Admission	102
Octogenarian	103
Death in Room 20	104
Katrina's Couch	105
The Doctor's Wife	106
The Ashes	107
November North America	108
On the Death of a Friend	109

The Way Back:
Beyond Suburbia

Continent

Hands outline the shape:
Australia's east west bulge,
the belly undercut.
The tip of Yorke
points north a millimetre drift
of unimagined time,
south, a triangle
the continent has dropped.
Islands fleck the giant coast
this land that hugs the downside of the world
between the ice and sun.
Explorers
eager for old loins,
spend semen in her salt.
The lips of Spencer Gulf
hang with exploitation.
Immigration consummates
her tired sand
her shape
familiar as a lover's arm.

The Glasshouse Mountains

They rise like chessmen on a checkered land
or hanging rocks where picnics end,
pocked with darkness,
Beerburrum, Coochin, Tibberoowuccum,
Tunbubudla, Tibrogargan, Coonowrin,
Miketeebumulgrai and Beerwah,
eleven ancient men of stone
frozen to the landscape of a crime,
boomeranged and broken by a father's rage,
symbols now to tourists
but known to Kabi people in their dreaming
as place of evil spirit north of bora ring and
Ninghi Ninghi. Aptly Kabi-named but
'Glass House': homesickness misplaced on foreign land
by Cook, then Flinders, in their Englishness.
They change at every angle
a trick of compass points to show their many sides
shawled in vegetation, haunted still,
volcanic plugs of time no one remembers.
Remote, apart in place,
the mountains tell of murder with a ravaged face
and brood.

Train Song

The train knifes through
its one way street
a song of green and blue
past idle towns, eroded earth
umbrella trees octopused with fruit
ghosts on empty benches
past stilted homes burrowed from the sun
stylised graffiti
stands of needled pine
shadows on the grass rush past
people on the move
clatter of the iron hooves
the whine of wind
wire flicking past
rifle fast
and in the twilight
silhouettes.

Boobook Owl

A double hoot stirs the edge,
distant, gentle and resigned.
Boobook calls the night,
defender of a space.
It little knows the peace to day-worn people
hoots can bring, mystic bird with wing
adapted for the kill.
Eyes torch the dark
discs surround
directing sound to eagerness.
Talons wait.
Mottled, tawny, small
hoot hoots again its wild call
on edge of sleep.

Bush

Boots in the wardrobe
suggest you

I carry a notebook
to pin you on paper

Words an obsession
or is it possession

seek what you mean

A walk in your space
like an exile, home

You are my refuge
from self and the city

A lover of sorts
a track for my body to follow

You are my fear
tamed as you are

on the edge.

Kangaroo

He eats forbidden grass
and populates fragility
but some will see him differently,
this cliché of a nation,
exotic to outsiders.
There's magic in the tail,
the tripod stance, the pouch,
the pogo gait matched to distance,
in ears that periscope for sound,
the deadly claw. Fine-limbed and mute
he owns a body he can stall
to suit a season.

Country Road

Two ruts in grass
Going and coming I know not where.
I long for the earth
For the grey weathered rails
Framing the gate and the chain
The squaring of land with wire
For the silence of grass
For somnolent cattle
Heavy with idleness
For the suddenness of birds by water
For the smell of dust
For space as defined by a line of trees
And light as measured in shadow
The giving of colour and form
For the promise of road
Over the hill.

Fruit Bats

Night-ridden
obscenely winged,
weighted down with skin too smooth and black,
on bones too big
they flap and crash in branches,
Archaeopteryx come down,
their clumsiness
proclaiming they aren't birds.
Consigned to air
they shriek their rights.
eating, sleeping, mating on their heads.
They live an other life
from all mammalian kind,
desiccated husks
on morning's ground
the only sign that they exist,
foreign fox of myth.

Lychee Madness

An ecstasy of lychees
in scrotums on the tree
pale at first, then pink
deepen in their skin
roundness in perfection
white and succulent within
they burst with juice against the teeth
a gluttony of lychees
eaten well beyond the need
their rough, red, hollowed skins
the only sign of our excess
like prawns' discarded shells somewhere
forgotten and enjoyed.

Flood

Rain drums a blackened land,
pummels years of dust to mud,
slaps the sheds and fattens creeks with swill.
Naked boys ride turbulence in dams
wild with the force of water.
Colours drain away,
night and day are mixed in grey
and needled rain.
An inland sea makes islands of the cattle,
rivers of the roads
and chases snakes to lonely heights.
The land's baptised
by fire first and then by flood,
paid in blood.

Outback Landscape

These are the leather people
fox faced, with creekbed skin
and hands like roots.
Heat and light suck at their land.
Litter forked in trees
suggests a flood
mocked by drought.
Plants withdraw
armoured in their leaves.
The deep egg waits.
Trees straggle
hair on old man's skin.
Earth shrinks to honeycomb.
Stone and sand
conference the land.

Christmas Bells at Mooloolah

From mute scrub wallum
ring the Christmas Bells.
Orange yellow voices shout the gray green
silence down, stalk the treeless clearing
on their slender notes,
shock with gladness his dry heart
beating through the bush.
He waits for echoes,
oaring flight of yellow tail
quail that spurt and cluster on the track,
the bizz and fuzz of insects.
Bells repeat their evanescent colour cry.

Brush Turkey

At dusk he penetrates our yard
flopping over fences, scavenging,
stalking rails with stilted legs,
giant lizard feet,
yellow wreathed, and red.
Undertaker bird,
living on the fringe,
target for the stones of boys.
Absurd in flight, he blunders into trees
too big to perch, a feathered sack
made for ground not air,
user of what's there,
scratcher of the mound.

Heat Wave

Cicadas pulse,
plants hang limp
shade gives no relief.
Hot even in the dark and sheetless night,
we wait for nudge of cooler air.
We live slow motion.
Skin discovers sweat.
Outside heat is inside heat,
water, now a sacrament.
Cars become a killing field
seatbelts brand the hands.
People wear as little as they dare.
They joke of frying eggs
on roads, buying shares in ice.
Memory is lost of ever being cold.
Couples lie apart in bed,
desire put on hold
and dreams, when sleep does come,
find no haven.

Monaro High Country

Stones hold secrets.
Trees writhe from soil
high on hills that lie
as sensuous as thighs
where stars are mustered.
Sheds house the obsolete.
Tyres, chain and wire
drums and rusted iron
state the junk of country living.
The dog like liquid red
weaves the flock to thistled ground
that bleeds for rain.

Cockatoo

He throws a sulphur shout
smooth and seamless cream,
no hint of feather.
Claws curl like hands to beak.
He struts with self-importance,
the bird a nation
pins its reputation on
polkadots the air with fantasy
yet just a clown upside down
eager to show off
a screech like fingernails
across the blackboard sky.

Drought

Water's known by absence
in a ravaged place.
Earth contracts, cracks like lips
the empty space that was our land,
spills its dust to Air
to land elsewhere.
Fire follows last,
prepared for and allowed by all that's come before.
Men scrabble at the orange line,
a black, silent space behind
grey and birdless crater.
Strange hope to know what's been
will interrupt with green
retell the story later.

St. Andrew's Cross Spider

Unmoving
save for lifting wind,
she lies astride her crucifix,
nailed to her own artifice.
An altar jewel
poised in prayer, waits
patient as the season.
Unsuspecting insects blunder in.
She springs,
her jaw and legs begin arachnid work,
fang and turn the feebling moth,
weave in love's embrace
with semen silk that leaves no trace.
Her anal thread entombs the living dead.
She preens, and draws
in final stillness, juice with straw,
the bundled moth sipped to non-existence.
Again the spider lies astride her crucifix,
her name.
Her clutch of grey cocoons
ornament the web,
disgorge a cloud of teensie eyes on teensie legs
in rows, unmoving. Disturbed, they spread,
a scurried wave of minute monsters,
testament to spider love.

Letting Go

When he died she sold the house
glad to leave reminders,
with it sold the marriage
all his stubborn loneliness
the carpentry unfinished
the punishment to keep her home
for work was what there was, not going out.
Her body knew the floors and windows
cupboards, clothes and shed
the long straight rows of vineyard,
knew the money kept
the making do with what she had
and swept by sudden lightness drove for miles
letting go her breath.

Yellow-tailed Black Cockatoo

Drawn by water and the casuarina nut
they smack with size,
an eagle or an owl's weight in feathers
but with comic eyes.
They perch as though the bush was theirs,
not one but twos and threes
calling to each other plaintive cries
the sound of world in sorrow.
Their yellow cheek can penetrate the dark.
Beak and claws repeat their curve
of sturdiness, crest and moustache
breathe with mood. But all fall short
to wings that beat with length
and power when they launch,
a hit of yellow in the tail.
They rise and raft slow motion.

Men on Bikes

Bikes lean
stopped at cafes
where the men
hang out, brothers
bright as birds,
shorts that show
the curve of braided muscle,
sculptured thigh.
Who knows how far
behind them lies
the ribbon of their wheels
from years of sharing small talk
roads and sweat,
dawns, fatigue,
a spank of tyre on the wet.

Budgerigar

Long forgot the days of light and space
when thousands moved as one,
swarming into trees and billabongs
shaking air with shrillness.
No more the wild green
but captive gene-manipulated blue.
Now the cage his stage.
Moustachioed man
bustles with self-importance,
bats, bites with mock annoyance.
Absurd bird, preposterous parrot,
troubadour of silliness,
singing, bobbing, eyes gone white,
he inflates/deflates constantly
round confidence and fright,
a beak as useful as a claw
in all his posturing.
A nano sneeze, a feathered shake
defines this scrap of merriment,
This minute comic far from home.

Road Butterflies

They flicker and dart
yellow and lime
stop only to fix
metal as bright, as slight as themselves
migrating on
their reason to pass and be gone.
They signal the eye
as butterfly men
alight and depart
on an edge.

Mount Coolum

The monolith stands seaward
sloping down to cane fields at its base,
lengthening its shadowed flanks
like sphinx's paws.
It rises lichen-faced and vertical
to where it rounds the summit,
totem of the Sunshine Coast
a wink of warning red at night.
Coolum vibes a presence
natives would call sacred
old before the dinosaur, unchanging,
but to climbers hints hostility,
indifference to goings on around it.

Sea Change

A swimmer bites through sea
a line of air and water,
wave massaged and separate,
stick figure fixed on course
until below he finds
an inner space, and hovers over ranges
desert dunes, spurs to endless yellow plains.
There aircraft fish drift idle
as he drifts now
beyond the shore, unmindful.

Mackay

The yellow town blazes by a green sea.
The tide eats footprints on the sand,
a cat prowling.

Old and new lie uneasily together.
Tuscan high rise prick the flatness
of coastal plain and sea
where boats, marina bright, like seagulls rest

and homes with iron hats sit stolid in the heat,
latticed with neglect. Their stilts provide
cellars from the sun, and storage
for the junk of living.

Verandahs tell of time and cups of tea,
laundry, corner stores, the heat.
People stay put, make ends meet,
palms clack with fronds like ladders
as the day sleeps.

Jellyfish

Dreamheads dot the sea,
migrate transparently,
motionless in motion,
umbrellas in a story.
Humans dread their touch,
inert and cold,
lifeless as a severed limb.
They drift in honeyed slowness,
there, whatever shore
heap formless on the sand
drowned in air.

The Farmhouse

Held back from sea
the house belonged to land.
A two rut road announced it.
What had been farmed
gave way to summer home.
Centuries stood still
behind the windowed face.
Floor rose with
swell of ground, and fell.
Vines twisted in like tongues.
Stairs led ladder steep
to bedrooms bright with sun
and insect hum where children dream.
Crooked rooms ran on
past coloured walls, past chairs
hollowed by familiar backs,
sand and dirt tracked in on feet
that kicked off shoes for summer,
a comfort time where children knew
their parents only as their parents.
The farmhouse smell of
wood and linen, earth and mould,
plaster, pipes and country air
returned it pinpoint sharp
though time and human lack of care
have trashed it.

The Rescue

They swam their 2K route
familiar as the land that lay beside it.
Stroking in she made her first mistake,
took off her fins, expected sand.
The deepness there, the lack of ground
stirred a fear that held her trapped, one armed.
Relentlessly the waves foamed in....
How random, easy, unforeseen
to drown with life unfinished,
a day like any day
yet huge in difference.
Fins could kick her in
but she had not the strength
to bend, hold breath, pull on the clumsy shoes.
She let them go, signalled
she was done, alone, beyond the fight.
And then she felt the strength of skin,
arms that took her from herself,
propelled her in, now a little distance
to the sand, giving back the land.

Rock Pools

Beyond the casuarinas
further than the belt of sand
rock pools, cusps of sea complete,
wait for children
buckets and bare feet
to find what's unimaginable,
a model world spread out.
Waves have bowled them smooth
pocked the rock that
twists a mountain range
a toe and fingers place,
hunting ground for giants.

Mooloolaba

The concrete gorge of units
Zanzibar, Sirocco, Shangri-La and Surf
frame the mix and mull of people
finding fun. Bikes and dogs are tied
at coffee clubs where tourists talk.
Shops solicit happiness. Cranes
pierce the sky like toys.
Sexes jog as regular as dawn.
Across the esplanade
the sea lies undeveloped
keeps its mystery and ashes
a place the skin takes memoried in.

Snorkel

Ripples play on sand
in this other world than air
where simple things are miracles
and I can fly, hover, flipper sound
spouting from my snorkel.
Not just fish strangeness
seaweed sweep, or streaking minnows
that become as one
a twisting, turning silver wall,
or rivulets of warm and cold on skin,
but soundlessness, wordlessness of such a different place.
In all this light and fluid motion
comes a water madness,
prompting me to find again
places to dive in.

Ocean Swim

One event has brought these minds and bodies here
separate and same, old lady on the fringe
conspicuous with cane and broad straw hat,
babies, flanked by parents, in their prams,
girls with dolphin thighs, silent iron men,
layback youths who take their trophies
dumb before the microphone,
guppy boys and girls, narrow-backed,
don't think about, just do, what is before them,
sixties men, brass skinned with silver chests
will plough the waves and can be counted on.
Old women lean, still smart with bodies like redundant fashion
pull on their caps and wait.
Swimmers now stand out from all the crowd,
from stalls of drinks, the human glitter,
the blast of worn out banter on the mike.
All must meet the surf and prove themselves,
must separate for this. The gun cracks:
hurls the human waves of coloured caps to meet the sea
glittering its diamonds. Beyond the barrier of whitened manes
their bodies look like insects
stick-figuring their way around a course of orange tents,
each mind alone, bent upon the finish,
tested by the solitude, the deep, the roll and sway of water,
fear, each orange landmark brings them near
to what they'd left behind, half-disappointed
leave the green mythology, merge again
break the sand and run,
taking the salt love home on their tongue.

Ocean Race

Privately we live the swim
before the gun
sends our bodies to the front.
Resolve we knew
ebbs in foam.
Enmeshed in limbs
we separate
in element our own.
Never are we more alone
or satisfied than now
fluid light, progressing by
a course of orange balls,
part of sea and sky.
Shore confuses water
halts the onslaught of the waves
rears them back
to whitened face
that spits us to the finish line
exalted.

The Deep

Distorted hands rake bubbles
through a wall as blank as green
where ashes scattered but unseen
lie nameless. Limbs that know
solidity of earth
the ache of trees
the lung that welcomes breath
push now against the transience
of dreams. Imagination's fear
draws edges. Mountains lie
reversed in trenches further out
lurid spaces hands will never go.
Hands that weave the air
pause and let the mind supply
what may be there.

Seahorse

Slow moving S
fins forward on a different plane
an ornament on strings
unlike a fish
more lizard, monkey, horse in one
with swivel eyes, prehensile tail
and tapered head
reticulate and pouched
its tiny bang of birth
with replicas exploding out
like larvae to the sweep,
is camouflaged, but not enough
for people's lust for difference
and desire.

Late Love

After years of coming home
to her own image, meals alone
the narrow bed, they met,
the ease of their togetherness
all the more surprising
for her gypsy single years.
A sudden lightness found its way in talk,
in letting go what she'd had,
in planning two by two their country camps,
gardening their love in slower time.

Canberra in January 2003

Fire came as suddenly
as accidental death.
An orange front drove them out.
Some stayed and tried to save
from this new enemy, their ground,
refuge from the sky and street,
selections of a life half-lived,
their money's worth tied up in one address.
They watched it go,
the space their walls had shaped,
reservoirs of air in rooms
familiar as their hands,
memory and love locked up.
Gone and grieved, replaced by somewhere else,
a foreign place, unclosed,
exposed to all the harm a planet stores.

Delivery

Secret this growing
round the bone
unmindful yet
the shuttered eye
quiescent brain
thumbstruck
knowing only tightness
and the dark
a fluid sway
lowered towards the day
and unguessed light.

Not from choice they leave
their home, life-lined with cord
and pulsed with risk, for what
they can not know
the risk of air
unwrapped, alone
before the touch.

Pippa

Newborn perfect in her parts
asserts herself with voice
astounding for her size.
How can something minuscule
produce such sound
to deafen and to drown
whoever's in her radar space?
A cataclysmic roar unstopped
fierce until the teat is seized
clamped in tiger jaws
then silence as she drinks
a desert crawler's drink.
Eyes begin to glaze and close
but still she sucks
at last lets go defeated
sack-like until
a signal starts the round again.
Will Pippa be Prime Minister?
Or will the world
take and shake her
back to size.

Mystique

Little shows, the rest
is all that you suggest
the things you do not say.
Your enigmatic smile
shifts perception,
hints at love. You laugh
vulnerable though you are.

Upstairs Resident

Our house is home
not just to us
but to an upstairs lizard.
Immobilized by me
and me by him
we eye to eye
on carpet.
Rooms with cracks and crevasses
what luxury to hide,
a stock of bugs unready
for the enemy within.
Wary still but nonchalant
he doesn't move for feet
but scuttles down the hall
when danger's passed.
I like to think I share
with such a profiteer,
this Chief Executive
who keeps his fortune to himself.

The Way Back

The distance between us
can only be lessened
by silence, or lying limb close
breathing each other,
healing the wounds
of our difference,
repairing the damage
of being ourselves.

Marital

Joined in darkness spine to spine
they lie separate in mind
hemisphered apart
he thinks expenditure, and shares,
world cups, she of brevity
her friends, and Art.
Silence draws their bodies in
the love of skin on skin.
They turn and face
put words behind,
reduce the space
with simple truth.

Return

The still house waits
for the car, the step,
the turning of key,
his boot on the tile.
The days of his not being there
have built up a tension
different from tension of being together.
She dreams of his hair
smoothness of skin, the compactness of him
and he's there, the measuring eye,
the boot and the key,
miniature hands unfolding his clothes.

Yesterday's Bike Ride

The blue day lingers
after the gravel road,
the undulating hills,
the valley filled with cane,
after the country homes,
the cluck of fowl,
the scrunch of tyres
and always the road
spelling the heat and the distance,
suspended in dust,
cycling on, part of the day,
part of the sun,
part of the sweat, the dirt
and the land we've become,
taking it with us.

Palace Centro

Illumed faces are one face.
She shakes the coil of herself
for somewhere, sometime, someone else
polarized by plot and faces
in love with love and just desserts.
She threads her words to share
compare with someone else's
version of the truth
before the light dispels.

Stick Insect

The phasmid sways,
a guise of wind
as if a stick
is not enough,
fabricator,
simulator,
fantasy on stilts.
Dissembler of the truth
it frightens with its tumour mouth
or is it nose?
goes to twiggish lengths to hide,
phantasmagorical inside.

Bird of Paradise Flower

Bird of Paradise,
elegant and smart,
you hold yourself apart
from other flowers.
Your spareness shocks;
even in the dark
you are an exclamation.
Invisibly to us you move
but with the speed of light
from swollen pink-tinged bud
to full blown flower in the hour
of a camera's lens,
your stem like flesh to touch.
In life exquisite
but in death how dull and brown,
all orange gone,
a clutch of twisted husks
no hint of paradise before
or winged birds that soar.

Hummingbird

bee
of birds

hangs blurred
by wings

in air
a hum

of speed
unlikely

for its
size

ruby red
an iridescent

head
tongue-holstered

bird
so light

its cobweb
nesting site

and dollhouse
egg

a figment
like itself

imagined

Rainstorm

From silence drops that can be counted on the fingers, gather
swell and die away
before the wind stuns fish to fly
and birds to swim
sounding down upon the tin
a din to mindlessness…
horsemen on the hills of night…
gutters overflow with cataracts that
beat the backs of sudden boys
thoughts that match this giving and receiving
air and earth, fall short to
chaos and its birth.

Rainbow Lorrikeets

Not one but hundreds
vandalise the sky
ungulate like distant bees
robbing silence with their brush tipped tongue.
Suburban gangs of larrikins
flash their missile bodies
orange, red with purple head
breaking air with screech and squawk
deafening the tree at dusk
overriding human talk.
Pendulous on trees, like bats
they lick their nectar upside down
and droop, like Christmas balls,
their gait a mix of pounce and sag.
The feisty collared convicts
swipe with orange hooks
birds that dare take on
the rainbow bully.

Love Story

The old dog lies clipped of heat.
She leads his crabshell frame
unhurried round the tumbled block
of sunspent homes.
He licks at food, persuaded by her fingers
dreams again, but she remembers
all the pieces of their lives
from west to east across a treeless plain,
puppy days, the way he'd rear
and throw his weight against her
play the games they knew
the yards and houses shared
the loves he'd seen her through
the willing profile wedged into the car
the gait a spring surprising for such weight
his silent company outside.

On the Side

Teaching takes new meaning
with children on the side.
Bells don't call the role.
A fractured class is hunted down
to trace unfinished names on dotted lines.
Karen fits. Ben abuses.
John keys music theorem perfect.
Some are further out than these
who none can know: Marie.
Her name and shining hair belie a shadow space.
Only eyes and sounds
that stand for speech, betray.
Her neighbours know her well
with fondness that one has for sadness,
for that which does not change
but lives routine behind the
backyard fence on sunlit days.
Music pulls her into light.
She responds with dance:
an unco-ordination all her own.
Grinning is her language.
Expectation here adjusts itself
to children on the side,
a leap that targets not a fitting in
with those tall poppies of the public
but begins.

The Sausage Tree

An ordinary tree
disguised until
long hanging stems
with flower chains
that bloom at night
drop down to mess the ground.
Then phalluses descend
like silent chimes
arm-thick and pendulous they sag
unsought by salesmen or by birds
but marvelled at by passers by
who snicker at extremities
at African surprise
a comic tree
whose obvious absurdity
destroys the hope
a tree might have
to be taken seriously.

The Parting

Dog days are gone.
He lies a ragged line
and she released in tears
recalls the years,
his trot, the laughing glance
he throws behind, his smell,
the platter paws, clips his shin.
He offers no resistance,
slips the needle in
and holds the shaggy head
across the line.

Conductor's Lament

He faltered, stopped
mocked by weakness, lowered rod,
his once remembered orchestration.
Silence grew which music should have filled
and still he stood unable to find words
while people waited.
He introduced his piece
mourning loss of music
all he would not live in braided notes
that curled about expectant faces.

The Piano Player

The face is safe
behind the black
but when the hands
strike home, they let
dammed passion out.
A river breaks
with fluid sound
to plains of faces
willing to be drowned.
It circles heads, alighting
on a grief, a dream,
a hope let go – or just
a wonder that the flying
fingers do their high tech work
and bring the planet down.

Sculpture

What spiraled from his head
astonished eyes
like some strange caption
or a wild dream.
Not just its smooth and polished form
sensuous, organic,
rippling to where the mind would take it
but the colour painted on:
hues of pink and green,
a point of blue,
yellow, purple, red
smacked the eye,
said 'Yes' to cheerfulness,
this brightness like a child's
exploration on white paper
brushing out surprise
in rainbow hoops
that set the air in motion.

Fitness

His body spells a triangle
of muscle, bone and skin
in equilibrium.
A foot that waits to help the earth rotate
an arm that pulls through sea to quicken tides
and legs to cycle slipstream
in air that is his drink.
With stillness of the trained
his body hums.
Even in his sleep he dreams of motion.
His body bends to love itself,
living to the max,
so far from those two myths
age and death.

Sprint

Coiled, stop-watched, on the block
he hesitates,
waits for gun to crack
fire him to fifty metres,
forty seconds of his life
with none of him held back.
Sound lets him go
curves him to the water
and his race. He ripples
shadowed to the flags,
ascends and streamlines
toward the end, stitching water.
He snatches air in troughs,
machine like now, detached,
surprised by what his body offers
and reoffers
until a point where, wall ahead,
he breaks, unravelled. Something fails
that brought him here
but still he slides with weighted limbs,
driven now by thought
to close that final gap,
to face the clock
and measure.

Medley

Arrows in, consumed.
Dolphin now he weaves, breaks the surface,
curls, slaps and shoots the wall
back along the lane ropes, drinking air
angel wings on shattered water
oars the surface on his back
frog kicks, head butts toward the end
then comes home hard with free
to hit the wall.

Between

Occupied with journeys, longing,
drugged with night
I break on morning, a lid between
unfinished dream and statement.
Statement is the day,
night the myth to snatch me.

Beyond Suburbia

Suburbs speak geometry,
ownership fenced in,
pots keep plants at bay,
parks are organized and trim.
Playgrounds tell the children
where to play,
pools dictate a clean blue swim.
Dogs are civilized,
bark their claim
in all the blocks that line
a street the same.
Cars ferry owners into
even greater order
but carry those in need
to where the human blueprints cease:
a stand of trackless paperbark on heath,
sprawl of sand and sedge,
a spill of rock, tumbled gum
where unmarketed and still
the waters run.

At Taabinga Music Festival

In those yards of 1846
when phoenix palms were evidence of fashion
and meathouse, shed and wagon
framed the homestead
set adrift upon the lawn,
fringed by ghosts as silent
and as present as the stars,
their work still visible
and set apart from ours
in all our studied leisure
and pursuit of Art,
there in laden ground
the music took us and we drowned.

Eclipse

Shadow bites the sun.
People stare and disbelieve
the early dark, coming at a time
so out of joint, as though the laws
which order chaos stop
to let this bedlam in.
Birds are tricked and roost.
People gasp
their waiting justified,
'totality' a climax to the sliding bite
before the diamond ring.
Someone said 'describing it
is like explaining colour to the blind.'
'You feel a universal part.'
'The wonder…
all will balance on a number.'

King Parrot

Name's the thing: King.
It captures grace, stateliness.
Cautiously he drops
whistling a question
smacks the air with red
bright as blood
trouser-legged in feather
tail a train behind
in flight a slash of blue
as if there could be more.

.

Country on the Edge

Beyond a desertscape of tiles
lies casuarina country.
The blackened holes of rusted cars,
a twisted buckled gate
will not subtract the beauty
of its space. Minute flowers
prick with colour grey green land,
like limbs the white gums stretch.
Spider webs glint angled in the sun.
Birds squeak and trill
across the traffic's snarl. People
forked on bikes enjoy their version of
the land. Stands of stunted trees and sand
give way to wallum,
like an aching of the heart.
Trash decays. And just along
the long flat tongue of highway
licks.

Buff Banded Rail

Behind the infrastructure
corporate design
the traffic grid, the muffled roar
and all the signs of interaction
that is dubbed a city,
it appears,
occasional, elusive,
seeking food,
shy dweller driven in
that once would not be glimpsed
poking its slender neck
into dark spaces
lifting tripod feet
speckling the morning
with bars of black and white
with russet notes
flicking an interrupted tail
with jauntiness.

Inside Binoculars

Zero in
on micro world
enlarged
the pleasure shock
that detail gives
movie screen
for one
a love affair
cheating distance
for a closer look
a kiss, a knife,
feathers, eye,
all that passes by
unseen and furtive
in a private space
enclosed
part and yet apart
close, not close enough
Voyeur
who put his life behind
for this small room of time
enhanced.

Corellas

Cocky bright they lift and drop
alight on Casuarina trees
a scattering of white
drawn by puckered nuts
they clasp with lizard feet.
Swivel-eyed, they bore with rounded tongue
polkadot the green
turn the moment into fairy tale
a story read to children
rapt in words of snow white birds
smooth as cream
that hang and droop.
The quiet feeding stops.
Querulous, they rise
raft to other feeding grounds
bleat their sound of hundreds passing
fade and leave the morning.

The Prophecy

She dreamed her mother disappeared.
Searchers trawled the scrub
finding only space she'd left behind.
She saw her mother's unpinned hair,
discarded shoe; unable to find help
close in on circles of herself
without a landmark in her mind.
Finding her was not relief
but confirmation lost
where all the dogs and searchers
could not find.

Flying

With noise and tension of a thousand drums
the predator lifts off
to where the sun slides by
dragging night unnaturally behind.
Dark hunches down
'til morning lights the cabin
to its dream of height.
Sun and stars forever shine unclouded.
The engine comforts with a muffled roar
before the bird descends.
The altimeter falls as we return slow motion
glad to be where life needs no support,
for more prosaic ground,
the hawk at gate.

Trans Pacific

The blue curve
known as sea
hints infinity
to boundaries of skin
the pettiness of flesh
the narrow range of temperature
sound and light lived in;
arms and legs no match for this
enormity; it cows the mind with
vacancy and speed. A solar touch
stirs in landed days ahead unease
in dreams, breaking up of reason
a supersonic flirt with time
countries swapped like marbles
arriving just as though
this cheat of distance never happened
but for mind.

747

metal bird
bug-nosed
lumbers on the ground
splits space
inhabits grace for air
stirs an ancient riot of the blood
miracle of parts
neighbour to a star
transports an idle crew
romance for some
suspended as they are
from drag of earth
and daily lives
before they're back
from where they've come.

Subterranean

Below the planet face of dirt fall zones,
layered down they trench a solid sea to evolution's showpiece:
jaws, teeth, bone, shell and broken stone
diluvian, the frozen ripple of an antique shore
unchanged today, seams of coal and quartz
thrown back, iceberg rock submerged,
a mountain range lies drowned,
and water rubs a vault for eyeless fish.
Higher still beneath the face
stick men lie in rows of little rooms
or piles of them heaped as one, too shallow to keep secret
the detritus of war does not lie deep.
Closer still, unsecretive, unfeared, beneath the grass façade,
last year's bottles, tins, plastic, metal bits
make their skin deep statement.

Jetlag

An elephant body doesn't forget.
It knows when it is pushed through zones of time.
When destination clocks strike ten
the body strikes the time it knows
way back then, waking unappeased at two am.
Not just time the body knows, but home,
a word that conjures all there is of love,
all there is to write about and die for,
set in contrast by another place,
achingly familiar. And yet arrival makes me stranger
to the place I knew the best.
I travel on in dreams, transit takes me over,
always checking in, looking for what isn't there
a figment of the air. I wait for time to close the gap
and find me.

Summer House

Rafters were her climbing bars
in rooms that pooled with ocean light
where horseshoe crabs like armoured cars
tided in and out. Her feet knew rock
and know it still. Boulders formed a floor
housekept by waves, a garden shore
where water lapped her dreaming.

The Grapes of Childhood

Long before remembering
but not before desiring
hung grapes in neighbourhoods
vertical beneath the leaves
and shared with bees,
purple, heavy sour-sweet
like wine made flesh,
there to be discovered,
shaped for children's hands.
Forbidden, we ran wild
stained with juice and ready for the chase,
seeds and vines behind
to tell an angry neighbour
of our raid.

Aged

It's not her face
or half-light truth she
builds her fiction on,
the cup that doesn't reach her lip,
the food she won't consume,
her stolen clothes,
the eyelid closed between us,
not the time she multiplies by ten
to do the smallest act
but her sparrow back,
the smallness of the shoulder blades,
the vertebrae so close to skin
is what brings in
her age.

Depressed

The bright balloons of her
the timbred laugh, the ease of motion
are as nothing. Like a rock
he lies unchanged,
unreached, his face impervious
to thought or action,
a body unremembering to move,
uncaring. Silence yawns between them,
lingers while she turns
and waits.

My Mother's Rooms

Room by room she conjures
up her life, and time,
staircase, hall and pantry,
secret places children own.
The day the horses brought old Harry home
slung between their necks.
The warren house on cliffs,
porch of early love.
Her life unfurls
peopled by her family
now themselves inheritors of houses.
House by house
remembering their light,
she dreams her rooms at night,
defense against the day
where age proclaims its narrow rim
to hold her in.

Obese Woman

She props on the bed
baring her buttress thighs
a landslide of flesh.
Shoulders like ski runs
slope to her gut
roll to the hills of tapering legs
tipped by dependable feet.
Inside sea caves slide.
Gravity hugs her to earth
like a cross.
The landscape moves
displacing air with grace
cleaving space to
whatever port or narrow strait
she's headed.

Lady with Oxygen

Movement defeats her
depletes her of air
that life in a bottle
laid in her frame
she pays for like bread
and replaces. She knows
what's enough and ignores it.
She's learned to be tough
to wait out the siege,
exhaling in whispers,
to weather the tremors
the practice in dying
drowning in air
just to be there with the rest.

Hierarchy

In a crochet of tubing
marshalled by monitors
and all the apparatus
of measurement devised
to watch an illness
she lies still undiminished
though her face is masked
and knows that when it
comes to grit love loses,
sex, status, food and shelter go,
knows as divers know
their life compressed to moments,
only air.

Perspective

She, who thinks she's old,
looks young to those who are.
Her bare legs stir their memories
a surge they had forgot,
something fresh brought in,
shielded as they are
by safety, meals and central heating.
Too young they say she is for children of that age,
so far to go, and yet she knows how near.
She plays the game she's young,
as they play how they're old.
The game allows some looseness with the truth.

Old Man Dying

The old man lay
his face like wax
a spectre who surprised with conversation,
movement when he chose.
His daughter sat,
an echo of his face,
not knowing how to deal with silence
or goodbye, being there together,
what to say of lifetimes
reddened in her eyes,
uneaten food carried in and out
by nurses doing jobs
that can not matter,
feeling what's unspoken.

Night Patients

Darkness enters rooms
with blacked out windows.
Patients lie between
reality and dream
anaesthetised by night
as uniforms in torchlight
measure charts
untwist the tubes
that tie a body to disease.
Cold and soundless
night's a country
we return from
slung between our sleep.
We wait confronted by ourselves
for daylight's point of view.

Surgery

Weighed and gowned
surrounded by expectancy
and orders
the walls of cheerful faces
forms and flowers,
he waits hour upon hour for a blade to break
the sanctity of skin
and find his deeper self
and once that danger's passed
in false relief,
the unexpected aftermath.

Hospital Admission

A small self
holding his heat
privately
offers his body
to eyes
grateful for tact.
How humble his underwear
here. His T shirts defenceless,
his blood's nameless fear
recorded on paper
in waves of a question.
He holds to a pillow,
to the option of hope.

Octogenarian

The letting go is slow, unnoticed
'til a word betrays the crooked frame
who up to now deceived himself as well.
Suddenly the secret's out.
He seems surprised you know
what anyone would know,
asks again, repeats,
becomes a gentle fool
with packaging his party hat
a stab at truth his cane,
the lightness of his being
we're too young,
too sensible to catch.

Death in Room 20

How dead a dead man looks
propped up in life's last minutes
snoring air, even then
harried by the tests,
technicians with their orders.
The Health Machine treats all as one.
The stillness stuns.
The breath that's not a breath
exhaled from lungs, the years let go.
The mouth a hole,
the plastic face,
the eye where nothing is,
the torso once to its own living shape
now straightened out
willing to be moulded.
Inhuman or too human?
Before the void nurses pause,
hesitate with sheets then
leave the face exposed
shielded by the door's red sign
Do Not Disturb,
the cover up, the question
as to who's the one disturbed.

Katrina's Couch

The couch was safe, a harbour to sail into,
moorings masted by her intravenous pole,
lined by times where she'd survived before,
caught her breath from drowning.
A couch can't change as she had changed.
Its view remained the same.
The room assured her of a former life
and still a life to come, as she lay still,
islanded in illness,
waiting for the pattern to repeat.
She held herself in check
guarding those resources where she bought her time,
savouring the feel of linen and the air around.

The Doctor's Wife

She loved him most
when he came home
worn with patients' stories,
tired by their load of fear.
He looked at hope and listened,
told them straight and
when he didn't know,
about his eye a lightness,
something to go on with,
his stethoscope a noose about his neck.
In the clothes he dropped
she smelled the polished floors,
the betadine, the lights, monitors
and beeps, the drapes, the swinging doors,
the soulless presence of equipment.
They had no need to talk,
to sit and watch the sun go down,
enough.

The Ashes

Though the sun blazed
and children played on sand
this day was not like other days.
Though fathers held their children
shoulder high through surf
this day was not like other days.

We bore our flowers out
treading water silent
watched the sky for what we knew would come.
The moment grew
insect like in distance first, then high
noisily above the spreading circle of our flowers,
thwacked the sky.

The ashes arched against the blue
trailing like spent fireworks
puffs of rust red dust dispersed through air
so light they blew and spread
and settled where our grief would have them,
there, an open sea,
a flourish at the end, as she had lived.
This day was not like other days.

November North America

He knew a land
embraced in bark
statement stark as
change of season.
Sticks as bare as bone
hem in the winter sky.
Tides of leaves
that lie in drifts like snow unmelted
scrape and heap their endings.

On the Death of a Friend

Between us
talk has lost its relevance.
Your world is unimportant.
Sleep is what there is
to get you through.
Let me feel you there:
what you've done and said,
the shaft that was your humour
too late for that to matter.
We kiss our fairy tale goodbye.
I go with promises.

Strange reprieve
where death will pause
leaving you defenceless.
What future can there be in bones?
You who should be dead
whom everyone had given up
assert yourself
with this small space
to live again.

After hope-despair
you are another person.
Eyes to see, skin to feel
you've grown to such importance.
You know what love can do
and in your knowing go.

Also Available from BeWrite Books

www.bewrite.net

Shaken & Stirred – Poetry from the Far Corners

'*Poetry does not belong in the mind. It belongs in the soul and in the bloodstream. Shaken and Stirred proves that brilliantly. This is a collection with great potential and one to which a reader of modern poetry will want to come back for inspiration, again and again.*'

Nicholas Cobic

ISBN 1-904224-85-7

A Moment for Me by Heather Grace

A journal with poetry and photos by Canadian poet Heather Grace.

Decorated with poems about learning to relax, letting go, overcoming heartache, falling in love, parenting, even practicing yoga on the beach and photos of serene moments in nature, this journal is the ideal gift for someone who seems to have everything.

ISBN 1-904224-96-2

Letters from Portugal by Jan Oskar Hansen

Jan Oskar Hansen's attitudes are evident in his poetry: his wish that people were kinder and gentler; his abhorrence of war, his sense of humour about the senseless things people, including himself, have done.

There's something for everyone here – even those who aren't frequent readers of poetry will be moved by Hansen's passion, amused by his sarcasm, and delighted by his ability to paint pictures of the simple things in ordinary life – making them extraordinary.

ISBN 1-904492-20-7

sexions by Renée Sigel

From continent to continent, Renée Sigel's poetic insights will echo over landscapes and divides.

"Renée Sigel is one whose place in time, love of language, and clarity of eye has produced a poet with work that stands among the best of her generation."

Roger Humes

ISBN 1-905202-02-4

Routes – Twelve poets. A road less traveled.

Fresh poetic gems from today's wordsmiths. This sparkling new anthology is a rich expression of 21st century world culture and perspective. With more than 150 works from twelve contemporary talents. A dozen *Routes* to the beauty of truth.

Includes works by Tony Lewis-Jones, Jan Oskar Hansen, Dazz Jackson, John G Hall, Heather Grace Stewart, John Thomson, Clive Warner, Kathryn McL Collins, Paul Morgan, Heather Bryant, Tom O Campbell and Andrew Proudfoot.

ISBN 1-904492-60-6

The Vinegar Moon by Donna Biffar

"... in *Vinegar Moon*, readers are led along the paths and carried by the currents of truly remarkable writing."
             Wayne Lanter, Author of Canonical Hours

Pick up Biffar's *Vinegar Moon*, and discover a whole new world that lies beneath.

ISBN 1-904224-35-0

listen to the geckos singing from a balcony by tolulope ogunlesi

Tolulope Ogunlesi is a real discovery, a young poet of talent and enormous potential. This is his first collection of poetry.

... witty and engaging; a promising first outing by a poet with a clear, precocious voice. A truly significant achievement.
  Niyi Osundare, Overall Joint- Winner, 1986 Commonwealth Poetry Prize

ISBN 1-904992-84-3

The Drowning Fish by John G Hall

Already a staple in multiple literary publications, John G. Hall's poetry is a stunning contemplation of both the mundane and the extraordinary.
 With his debut collection, Hall makes an undeniably strong impression, experimenting with images of religion, elements, horror, and everyday life in his reflections on the world and the people within.

"John G. Hall's poetry has the gritty edge of a contemporary visionary in active development. This is an important book by one of England's most important younger poets." **- Jack Hirschman**, author of Front Line-Selected Poems

ISBN 1-904492-80-0

Printed in the United States
42768LVS00001B/127-135